About the Author

Rachael Lee was born in 2001 in Iowa City, Iowa, and grew up in Houston, TX as the eldest daughter in a large family of doctors. A rising poet, she began writing at a young age and would go on to publish her first book "No Exit" at nineteen before going on to major in English at the College of William and Mary.

No Exit

Rachael Lee

No Exit

Olympia Publishers
London

www.olympiapublishers.com
OLYMPIA PAPERBACK EDITION

Copyright © Rachael Lee 2023

The right of Rachael Lee to be identified as author of
this work has been asserted in accordance with sections 77 and 78 of
the Copyright, Designs and Patents Act 1988.

All Rights Reserved

No reproduction, copy or transmission of this publication
may be made without written permission.
No paragraph of this publication may be reproduced,
copied or transmitted save with the written permission of the publisher,
or in accordance with the provisions
of the Copyright Act 1956 (as amended).

Any person who commits any unauthorised act in relation to
this publication may be liable to criminal
prosecution and civil claims for damage.

A CIP catalogue record for this title is
available from the British Library.

ISBN: 978-1-80074-645-9

This is a work of fiction.
Names, characters, places and incidents originate from the writer's
imagination. Any resemblance to actual persons, living or dead, is
purely coincidental.

First Published in 2023

Olympia Publishers
Tallis House
2 Tallis Street
London
EC4Y 0AB

Printed in Great Britain

Dedication

To Milton Zuanic, who heard a tree falling in the forest when nobody was around.

1

No exit

It was in that first glance
you sat down, not quite winded
on a day with no clouds
in a coffeeshop that morphed to fit you in
like the last piece of a collage
and you looked right into my patchwork soul and

pulled me over some steep edge where I find myself now
out of the corner of my eye I see you peering
hesitating at first, we flick away and back
before those eyes are all I can see in the world
swelling up to fill my view like a supernova
and sight distracts me from the freefall
our hands find each other effortlessly
and we inch closer and closer until I can feel your breath
like wind on my red blushed face
all it takes is for your gaze to drop for a millisecond
for our quick trap hearts to catch the other's and
explode as we crash together

Night

Night falls
she dips down
to scoop sugar stars
from a pure black bowl
sprinkles them
into her milky whey
her dark wind
blows air into my lungs
and I am not the moon

in the vast expanse of her sky
she's halo-ed by a yellow iris
as the last rays of daylight
stretch to touch her dark skin
to frame her long hair.
Like a raven,
I press against her darkness
hoping to find refuge
in her camouflage

"Icarus's Lament"

Sometimes the light hits you just right
and the music fills my lungs before I exhale smoke through my nose,
the light touches your skin like a spotlight as I lean in
refracting a golden halo around your head
turning your eyes to amber
and letting your honey heavy lashes drip closed
as we dive headfirst into each other.

Sometimes you reach out and touch me just right
your fingertips burn into my skin like a stencil,
they form twisting vines and tight patterns along my waist
and I'm flush against you and it's never been so hot.
Your flash flare kiss ruminates against my mouth
and the freefall as you push against me only lasts a second
before I'm caught by my wings, those vices –
they encircle me with their white-hot light
and singe your fingerprints into the soft flesh of my back.
My candle wick skin craves you it does.

My mouth is still white-hot with your searing kiss,
my body still branded with your handprints…
I can't help but fall for you.
My face turned up into the bright iris of the sun
as I plummet into the earth like a wax meteor
my skin, my hair, my paper-poem heart
all singed with the flash-flare image of you
and I know I would melt all over again
for you.

The Future

When I'm with you the future speckles behind my eyes
like light seeping through an open window
when I'm with you the future is so fucking bright
like the dazzling spotlight as I face an audience of you
or the first flash of a firework
and it's devastating.
It burns a hole into my paper-mâché heart
the light means death to me
it feels like daylight creeping over a Monday
like the bright flash of an atom bomb
or the headlight of my father's car pulling into the driveway
The light at the end of this tunnel terrifies me
the rattle and hum of the rail beneath us
the steady increase of the two wide headlights
I stand with my back to the train, facing you
I know there is no exit
and yet, you shine like one
two dark eyes flash amber with the light behind me
EXIT, they tell me, EXIT

When I look at you, I see that spotlight
and I know there is no happy ending in sight
but I hold onto these last moments of darkness
the precious seconds before the house lights go up
I know that when you look to the future
the prospects are so bright they burn your eyes
I know the glow is so much that is sears your irises,
even with your eyes closed.
I know you are frozen in the headlights, staring at the sun
so when I tell you that I love you
I know all you can see is the blinding light behind me
the headlights of the oncoming train
the bright finale of a supernova sun
all you see is the light at the end of the tunnel

I wonder if it frames my face the way it illuminates yours
when I tell you I love you I feel that gold halo grow around me
the heat of it against my neck
facing you, I see in full lighting the fear in your eyes
the paralysis as I beg you to look at me instead
when you finally do look at me
I know part of you yearns to tear your eyes away
from the black abyss that surrounds us
and right into the yellow pupil of the train
the bright mouth of death

I know soon the speed of the train will be audible
the light will encompass us and smother us out
the sun will rise and put an end to our perfect day
and as I look up into your eyes, swallowed by the light and wind
I know that it's truly too late for us.

Haiku (Portrait of a Lover)

the birds fly onward
but I am stuck, eternal
as a paperweight

heart worn on my sleeve
bloated and crying and ripe
ready for eating

the taste far out rates
the growing pile of plates
that lie before you

I'd gladly rip out
rip out my own heart if only
to watch you devour

my paperweight heart
ties me to you and keeps me
from flying onward

I fell in love on a tuesday

Hey moon,
hey dark-skinned fool, hey bright mouthed June
I love you and I crave a boon

for when I look up in your sky
and see your shadows pass me by
I am but a patient etherized upon the table

so let me love you if I'm able
the way a horse may love a stable
or how a ship can love her anchor

and how the werewolf loves the moon
or how mirages cling to dunes
I'll love you however you may choose

because I know that if I lose you
my perfect soul, folie a deux
I'll wind up losing myself, too

so, does the moon define the sea?
does the ocean need the beach?
did he who made the lamb, make thee?

as werewolf sings his "goodnight, moon"
and ship will cut her anchor loose
I'll wish I had just one excuse

for why you left so suddenly

Moonlight

my heart aches
like a thousand wing beats
they flutter against my bruised chest

I dreamt of kissing you
but in reality, I know you are one for the wind
I fruitlessly reach out to hold onto you

my fingers lose their grip in your long hair
I might as well be reaching for smoke
the curve of your hip, the smell of your perfume

they haunt me as I cannot reach you
as you leave me in this place with no exit
I try and follow you regardless

it's like pinning both my hands against your watery chest
desperately trying to keep you against the sand
as the moon pulls you back into her awful embrace

Two blue-sky metaphors of you

skyline

Sometimes the whole sky seems to darken
as if your shadow reached over
and hid every cloud, every drop of sun in the sky
and I have to ask atlas to reach the highest apples
just to get a glimpse of you

It's you I imagine, you know,
you I picture leaving me to hold up the whole world
with just my two hands and a pen
you who leaves me for dead
and down here at the foot of this great world
the sun burns so hot that in a moment of weakness
I wish I was under your shadow again

Birdbrain

In Galveston, the old Victorian houses paint their roofs blue
so that the birds think it's the sky
and don't plant their nests along the windowsills.
When you told me that you thought you might love me,
I was a robin in the blue, blue sky
in the cloudy expanse between the freckles on your cheek.
I thought that I was free to fly,
a baby bird who found herself beneath a fresh layer of paint,
who never knew the sky had changing clouds and breeze,
who thought that the nails and screws
were just stars in the ever-blue painted sky

Icarus and his White-Hot Sun

I suppose this isn't a bad way to go.
The firework display of burning feathers falling around me
and the smell of ash and flesh outlined with your red singe.
The mayfly nosedive towards the ice-cold earth
turns me to a lucifer lit up against the dark sky.
My skin crisps and tongues of fire lick up my back
and I look down at my two hands to find I was never truly
human.

I never even got to know you.
Before you spat your sparks into my hair
and turned my outstretched arms to tinder.
I am utterly unrecognizable.
Your fingerprints scorch me even now
the feeling of your hands against my body like salt in my
wounds.
I wake up in the midst of sleep
with your phantom hands against my mouth or my neck.

Your hungry fingers digging into my thighs and my hips white fucking hot against my fragile skin.
I am not paralyzed as I once was, no, instead I leap from the coffin,
from the bed that encases me and run.
I run as if I am still alight with your fiery touch.
I stand there naked, letting the ice-cold water run over me washing the flames down the drain
scrubbing the ash from my hair
slowly reforming my waxy face into someone I can recognize.
At the time I thought I couldn't survive without the fire,
but I'm finding it's even harder to survive with the burns.

Hometown

The salt cuts my skin
the waves lick my ankles
somehow it still feels like I'm running away
I'm dreading the day this stops being home
our bare legs swing over the water
and our bare necks peer pale moon flesh
and I can't help but think to myself
"There really is nothing left of us"
somehow I find myself saying goodbye
to all my favorite places
closing doors that led to my favorite people
and allowing these feelings to become memories.
in reality, our hands don't connect like I'd hoped
your kiss is more awkward than ever
and I'm devastated to find
you're just another boy
meeting you was like the first time
I listened to my favorite song
kissing you was like the first time I ever saw the ocean
memories, memories
already I can't imagine the temperature.
saying goodbye to you was throwing away my favorite shirt
it was vacuuming sand out of my car
and looking at the sunset thinking to myself
that the sun managed to consume our last day

2

Spring

I can't help it
when I'm walking its heavy,
as if my bones were replaced
with long femoral dumbbells
like my blood is liquid glass.

Sadness weighs down on me
as if I have to push the sun up
and drag it across the sky to move the hour

I'm out of breath ten steps from my door
and I can't help but stare
at the bushes outside my window
the dark leaves are covered
by the new baby green foliage
the darker, older arms and fingers

That I saw bear the harsh winters and hurricane winds
find themselves overshadowed
by none other than the infant growth that knows nothing
how is it fair,
that the old leaves can make way
for a new start over a spring
and I'm still the same girl after all these years?

Ophelia

I find myself thinking of you often
because I see the future in your glassy eyes
the world crashed down around you
one wretched piece at a time
until nothing remained

Your death went unsung
maybe that's why I find myself singing so often
because otherwise I feel my lungs start to fill with mud
I start to feel my dress grow heavy
and my siren skin shrivel in the waves

How lucky we are, us Opheliacs
like mermaids, we swim after you
like Diana's tribe
I find myself itching for oceans of water
gasping for waves and waves of silence

My flowers wilt and die
but not before you do, Ophelia
and suddenly I am only left with dreams
and too tight clothes and shoes with no laces
and a clean white bed with whiter sheets

The tulips you gave me still rotting on the desk

A trophy room

Pyramus and Thisbe

When I die, promise me three things.
Promise to bury me beneath the mulberry tree
where in life I'd thought to lay forever, my ear flattened pink
as a flower pressed against the pages of your steady
heartbeat.
Say you'll turn spill me like wine onto the white flesh of the
berry,
and that the love you show me will forever join us in death.
Promise that you'll find me in an adjacent grave
and when the first silvery, cellophane moth
lands on the white, carved open portion of my wrist
to suckle milk and honey from our slick skin,
say that we can sleep in the shade of the mulberry
and let the pale larvae consecrate this marriage of ours.
Promise to meet me there before the sun sets. Bring your
sword. Bring my veil.
Skewer us like wine-grapes on a silver thorn. Bleed into my
open womb.
Smile as the syrupy sun settles onto your blonde eyelashes,
and wrap us in a blood-soaked veil to say your vows.

Pull out the sword who wears us like a wedding ring and stab it into the earth.
Tell me that you love me. Hold your organs in. Come into the shade.

Streetlight

Streetlights pass by me like fireflies
and the murky blackness is replaced by those orange eyes
at first. they're scattered, until they grow into a city
where the train slows to stop
as if the honey thick light was pulling on the wheels
slowing them as the train pushed through the thick
marmalade air

As we fly past a library, or a diner I imagine the fluorescents
are days and nights passing in front of me
town after town, separated only
by the ever-changing skyline of black trees

Just as quickly as we appear, we disappear
speeding past the last orange peaks of humanity
into the all-encompassing night

To the end,

I was born here
two steps away from the edge of a cliff named after you
waiting for the last call of the heron
or a particularly strong gust of wind

Letting this lifeboat carry me against the grain
knowing it would only take the smallest crash
for my small world to be jettisoned from the craft
I'm hugging my knees, and the captain is pointing

I feel their little smiling hooks dig into me
the long fishing line tying me to earth like a tent
if I needed, I know I could cut the lines of this emergency
parachute
and freefall to the earth like an Icarus

Voices call to me from over the cliff
but I am too afraid to even look.
I sit, rocking with my shutter-eyes shut tight against the wind
the feeling of hands against my skin overwhelming me

Their hands they pull me from the edge, but others push me
closer
I don't have time to think of moving towards or away
these hands, not my own, decide my fate
and it would only take one hard shove

it would only take one hard shove

Virginia Red

In daylight they're smoother
my little rivulets
more comfortable

that creamy backsplash
those rows of identical houses
Virginia red clay

little stretch mark
you might have always been there.
those paltry pink ghosts

sit line by line
they make their beds
and dust away the red sediment

little red tattoo
rosy stitch itch
might as well

be a mole or a hair
or a fingernail
that teardrop scar

makes red rain come down in sheets
those little soldiers
make me want to eat

my unripe apples
their unmarked skin calls me
to sink my teeth in.

No Exit (Again)

I'm no longer human
I renounced my womanhood long ago
and naturally the remnants of humanity, the fragments of
normalcy

that clung to me like smoke in my clothes
followed soon after.
It used to be that my emotions

clotted against my raw skin
like embers and ash, they burned me
they poke me and bleed me

those briars those thorns
they dug into my skin and said to me "it's true"
oh, I'd kill for just one more "it's true"

now the crow call sounds odd
the teacup round my thumb like a noose
too glass, too crystal

the clink of it against the spoon as alien to me as a China
man
as a father, as a man
the fit frame of my glasses nauseates me like a fishbowl

I see fellow passengers pass by me
and I begin to realize, how unlike I had hoped,
it is not this earth, not this matrix or sun surrounding it

that are the strangers here
but instead, me
the rings of light that frame my eyelashes burn into me

my microscope glasses fan these flames
the sounds of a life I cannot have surround me
crying, laughing, singing

they haunt me
they remind me there is no hope
and certainly, no exit

Plath

It's hot here
in the oven
the drag the pull

my fisheyes glaze
my pork rib skin
bubbles and crisps in heat....

some people say
well, most people say
to take her out

I say leave her.
Sure, we'll have
no more poems

the dripping faucet
that dried up vein
will never again

spit out those sticky pearls.
What do we do
to the broken machine?

Change the parts
and prescriptions
so it may keep pumping art

out of her rusted arteries.
Better yet, I say
is to let it decay

to let it find rest
in the junkyard
turn those poems to glue

take out the salvageable parts
and melt down the rest
in that industrial oven

I say leave her.
Nobody ever listens to me though, do they?
Instead, they'd

insist on pulling me out
hydrating my sandpaper skin
watering my tulips

those delectable cherries.
Tie her hands to the desk
press a pen into her palm,

give her space
enough to write
her pathetic poems

but not enough
to reach the other wrist
oh leave her in, leave her in

Dust to Dust

What a spite
what a spurn
to waste these 18 years

I'm quite aware
nothing gold can stay
but what of silver?

of copper, of tin?
better yet is to say,
even trash cannot stay.

Perhaps only Styrofoam
remains after the apocalypse
perhaps cockroaches

what's the difference?
When gold and garbage
both return to dust?

The unadmired diamond
is just another rock,
Paris just another graveyard.

Helen of Troy and I
look the same to the maggots
at least, I think so

A Pearl

Somewhere at the crux of the ice-bound River Styx,
you pulled me under the ink-wet waves,
opened your frozen mouth like a shattered sapphire,
and promised to baptize me with your love.
Your last breath slid against my body,
a bubble pressed white under the fragile skin of shore-ice,
as your fingers opalized against me
like a decade of rosary beads
forming white glaciers against our star-crossed corpses.
My fingers stiffened in the reeds of your hair
as our lazurite kiss crystalized with the Word of the Lord
and I prayed that God might accept the sacrifice at your hands
a sanguine covenant in the stiller, bluer lips of my lover.
In its mouth, an oyster will layer two pearls into one,
its spit calcifies over the two grains, one wet page at a time.
And like a two-wicked candle dipped into an indigo wax,
we're to freeze together on the midnight tongue of God.

Plato and I

tThe flames of the fire
burn my back
they sear their strange patterns into my eyes
mirages of lovers, of liars
of all the beautiful things in the world
they're all up there

splayed across the cave wall
flashing against my Sistine chapel eyelids
viciously flicking flames and shadows
like a Jackson pollack, like a splattering of roadkill

Plato and I
can't help but reach out
trying to feel the leaves of the trees
the taste of the wines
but the chains dig into my wrist and I cannot leave

to me, sunlight feels like fiery flames against my skin
as does moonlight
the cool drips of water feel like blisters
the black night feels like the sweat on my neck
it all feels of fire, fire, fire
all I know is fire, fire, fire
and there is no exit

Opus

They say in a fire
you look to your opus
that prized possession

so tell me then
why I only had eyes
for soft wrist flesh

that pure gold baby skin
the pull the tear
the krono's tongue

that razorblade
my sunken gaze
turned only to

caramel candy skin
those China doll arms
polyester dress

I dig my finger in
and pull out a plum
bloated and ripe

juice drips down
my sleeve-heart
I can't describe the taste

Momma,

I'm sorry.
I didn't mean to throw away your hand-knit sweaters.
Rip your self-stitched gown.
To spill red ink over your baby's doll-skin
when I opened her seams.
I promise I won't do it again.

I'm sorry.
I promise to treat it gently next time.
I won't cut down the garden that took all spring to bloom.
I promise I'll never again
try to press your newborn flower buds.
To ferment your fruits in frankincense.

I'm sorry momma.
I didn't know how much you cared for this creation.
How heavy I was to carry all these years.
How much blood you spilled to bring me here.
I didn't know how much you cared.
And for that I'm truly sorry, momma.

I wish I'd known how you pulled the sun down like an orange,
how you cut the sky into bite-sized pieces,
and smoothed the sea to tuck me in at night.
How you hand-wrapped the world as a gift for me.
I wish you knew how sorry I am, momma,
for trying to throw away that gift with both hands.

The Flood

Sometimes the high tide
sweeps in so quickly
I have to hold my head up with both hands
and even though the dark coffee flood threatens to
swallow me up
I just close my eyes and remember sunny days
I remember feeling so happy
so hot so dry that I would do anything for a drop of water
I try to remember that feeling as my feet are swept off the
ground
soon there's only an inch or two of air
between the waterline and this home's great iris
so I take my deepest breath and sink down
force my eyes to open
they adjust to the sting quickly
they've seen enough salt in their lives
down here is the eye of the storm
the calmness the drift
the wracking waves and the terrible thunder
rock me like a baby
and I wonder if this is really
such a bad way to go.
There is no exit in sight
and I quickly find myself running out of air
the momentary calm that the waves gave me is suffocating,

my lungs catch on fire and I start to burn
and cold water turns my toes to stone
I'm trying to swim but my useless limb refuses to comply
no matter
soon, soon the grave cave of a home turns into open ocean
my furniture releases her schools of fish
and picture frame turns to kelp
by the time I leave this house
a hundred years have passed by me
this happy home is swallowed whole by the great white whale
and as I begin to escape its tangles
the sunlight burns my cave creature skin
it is a welcome pain.
Before I start that surface swim, I look down
to find that I have also changed
my neck scarred with new gills
and my fingers webbed to match my mermaid's tail
the flood has changed far more than just this city
its changed my bones, my blood
on some far-off island I see people waving to me
those refugees
I swim to them but as I take a breath of air
as my fingertips touch the sand shore and my skin kisses sunlight
all I feel is fire
my body rejects this place
I am no longer meant for earth
my lungs are scorched
my skin is blackened and crisped
the sand is gritty knife on my baby beluga skin

I sink back down into the waves
take in wet, shaky breaths
sneeze air out of my lungs
and try to revert to some semblance of normal.
Sadly, I find that the flood has changed me beyond recognition
but this place I once called home is changed as well
and although I am totally new, I am still the same girl I was
I wonder
if both myself and my home have changed in equal measure
if we could still be compatible after all these years

Train

The train puts me off balance
like the heavy weights of a tightrope walker
I'm pulled towards the ground
and even if I stand completely still

the trees flying past me and the sunlight flickering
as if some giant was turning the lights on and off and on
remind me that I'm going hundreds of miles per hour
away from, or perhaps towards, some sort of exit

I fear I'll go crazy if I sit still
so I walk anxiously like a bride, down the aisle
for my safety, I'm told not to stand inside the vestibule,
I don't listen, closing my eyes and turning this train into a
hurricane

I lean on one foot and then the other,
allowing the train to lead me as if by a rope
I feel like an organ, blindly lead by some great force
some brain or foot who knows better than me

as I walk up and down the empty aisles
the wind whistling around the train encases me like an egg
the empty seats forman audience of none
each one grey and curved like a leather gravestone

the sickly-sweet perfume of the aisle pounds against my
skull
as I scrunch my eyes closed and turn this train into a
spinning top
or ballerina.
Into my own right shoe sliding against the ice,
or the embers desperately pushing through this cigarette
tunnel.